the ancient aramaic prayer of jesus

the ancient aramaic prayer of jesus

"the lord's prayer"

rocco a. errico

SCIENCE OF MIND COMMUNICATIONS
LOS ANGELES, CALIFORNIA

Seventh Printing—October 1993

*Science of Mind Communications wishes to acknowledge
Mrs. Marion Warfield Hefferlin
through whose generosity this seventh printing was made possible.*

Published by Science of Mind Communications

*Dedicated to all seekers
of truth.*

Preface to the
Science of Mind
Edition

The Lord's Prayer is perhaps the most widely known spiritual attunement in the Western world. Although this is an age when conventional religious expression seems lacking in any particular coherence, most people know something about one or another version of this classic and simple prayer. Even those who declare an antagonism to formal religious concepts are likely to be able to recite it from memory.

But how many people have any idea at all what it *means*? How many of those who self-confidently recite the comfortable rhythms have any slightest notion of what they are saying? And to those who do strive for understanding, what fullness of meaning is imparted by the familiar English words? What did Jesus, who gave this prayer originally in the Aramaic language, intend to convey? And how much of what he wished to share has been either obscured in translation or obliterated because the modern reader has no feeling for the overall cultural significance in the Middle East of such terms as, *Our*

Father, Hallowed, daily bread, temptation, evil, or even *amen?* These are important questions for those who look with deep respect at the teachings of Jesus, and who want to know what his prayer really meant.

Dr. Rocco Errico is particularly well qualified to provide answers, for he combines two special perspectives: he is knowledgeable in Biblical Aramaic, the language Jesus actually spoke; and he is thoroughly familiar with the culture of the Middle East as it was when Jesus taught there. Thus, Dr. Errico is equipped not only to bring the reader fresh translations directly from original sources, but he is also able to establish these translations within a cultural context that enlivens them dramatically. Drawing on his long experience as a lecturer, teacher, author, and scholar, he is able to provide a *feeling* for what Jesus was saying as the simple words of the Lord's Prayer were spoken. This is significant to the student of metaphysics, for it provides awareness that is uncluttered by theological considerations; and it also is important to the ordinary reader who is familiar with the Lord's Prayer but has little insight into its true meaning.

Science of Mind Publications is pleased to introduce Dr. Errico's book to a new and wider audience, believing that all seekers after Truth will be inspired by a modern examination of this two-thousand-year-old spiritual message.

2

PREFACE TO THE FIRST EDITION

Numerous volumes have been written on The Lord's Prayer. This book, however, approaches the prayer directly from the Aramaic language spoken by Jesus, his apostles and early disciples, and the people of his day. When our Lord taught this prayer to his young students and to the Aramaic-speaking people of Galilee, he uttered it in his own native tongue—Aramaic.*

The purpose of this small volume is to give the reader a clearer understanding of the overall significance of this famous prayer. It explains, in simple language, the meaning of the Aramaic words which Jesus spoke—what they meant to his apostles and disciples at that time, what they mean today, and how to apply Jesus' method of prayer in daily living.

This short, simple prayer contains eight attunements, or affirmations, which adjust one to spiritual forces in and around himself. This is how Jesus taught his disciples to tune in to the inexhaustible power of the heavenly Father, which is available to His children in every age. It is the way of peace, health, prosperity and understanding.

This book was written in answer to numerous requests to have in print some of the material from my lectures on The Lord's Prayer. May the reader find here a source of inspiration, and may this help him to increase his spiritual sensitivity, thereby strengthening his awareness of his union with our loving, heavenly Father.

---

*Later on, the apostle Matthew wrote his teacher's prayer in Aramaic in his own book, known as **KAROSOOTHA D'MATTAI**—"The Preaching of Matthew"

ACKNOWLEDGEMENTS

My sincere appreciation to Dr. George M. Lamsa, my teacher and Rabbi, who instructed me in the ways and habits of the people of the Near and Middle East and in the basic fundamentals of the Aramaic language. My appreciation also to Charles David Heineke, for his assistance in collecting and organizing my lecture material for this book.

All scriptural quotations are from the Holy Bible, translated from Ancient Eastern Manuscripts, by George Lamsa, Copyright © 1957 by the A. J. Holman Co., Philadelphia, Pa., and reproduced with their permission.

NOTE: The symbol, ⚕, which is used to introduce each chapter of this book, is a scribal abbreviation of the name of God as it was revealed to Moses on Mt. Sinai. (Exodus 3:14) It is pronounced *yah*. Ancient Middle-Eastern scribes employed this symbol to indicate that the writings or the manuscripts were of a sacred nature.

TABLE OF CONTENTS

5

PLATES

ܐܒܘܢ ܕܒܫܡܝܐ܆ ܢܬܩܕܫ ܫܡܟ ܬܐܬܐ ܡܠܟܘܬܟ܇
ܢܗܘܐ ܨܒܝܢܟ܇ ܐܝܟܢܐ ܕܒܫܡܝܐ
ܐܦ ܒܐܪܥܐ܇ ܗܒ ܠܢ ܠܚܡܐ
ܕܣܘܢܩܢܢ ܝܘܡܢܐ܇ ܘܫܒܘܩ ܠܢ ܚܘܒܝܢ܆
ܐܝܟܢܐ ܕܐܦ ܚܢܢ ܫܒܩܢ ܠܚܝܒܝܢ܇
ܘܠܐ ܬܥܠܢ ܠܢܣܝܘܢܐ܆ ܐܠܐ ܦܨܢ
ܡܢ ܒܝܫܐ܇ ܡܛܠ ܕܕܝܠܟ ܗܝ ܡܠܟܘܬܐ
ܘܚܝܠܐ ܘܬܫܒܘܚܬܐ܆ ܠܥܠܡ ܥܠܡܝܢ܇
ܐܡܝܢ܇

The Lord's Prayer in Aramaic

1
THE ANCIENT MEANING
OF PRAYER

The word for prayer in Aramaic, the language of Jesus, has a special significance. By uncovering the root meaning of the word, we can better understand The Lord's Prayer as we study it a line at a time.

It is very difficult, when going from one language to another, to retain the full impact and meaning of the original word. Something is always lost through translation. The task is even more difficult when it involves such vastly different cultures as our Western culture and that of the Middle East. This has been the problem in translating the Scriptures from Eastern to Western languages. So, before we examine the depth and meaning of The Lord's Prayer, let us clearly define the word "prayer" from the Aramaic point of view.

The Literal Meaning of "Prayer"

The word for prayer in Aramaic is SLOTHA. It comes from the root word SLA, which literally means, "to set a trap." In the East, when men went hunting, they would get a box, some bait, and a string. They'd tie the string to the box-trap, set up the trap, and then hide behind a rock or some other adequate shelter, still holding the string, and wait patiently for the animal they desired to trap. And when the animal came, they'd pull the string and catch the prey. So "prayer," then, literally means, "to set your mind like a trap and wait patiently to catch the thoughts of God"; that is, to trap inner guidance and impulses.

Other Meanings of "Prayer"

Prayer also means a state of mind where all thoughts are stilled and no attempt is made to project anything outwardly. It is an alert state of total sensitivity and attentiveness.

Another meaning of the word is "to make an adjustment," "to focus," or "to tune-in." A modern way to put it would be, "to select the channel" or "to set your mind on the beam." If I were going to speak to you in Aramaic, and were to ask you to turn on the television set to a certain channel, I would have to use the Aramaic root word for prayer. And it would mean, "to select the proper channel," "to adjust the set," or "to tune it in."

In prayer, then, we are adjusting and preparing our minds to *receive* God's "program." God is always "broadcasting." His "transmitter" operates 24 hours a day and never goes off the air. He is constantly beaming, sending, and signaling to everyone and everything in His creation. Infinite Intelligence is everywhere and in everything.

The Meaning of "God"

"God" sometimes is visualized as an old man with a long, white beard, dressed in dazzling white robes, and seated on a throne made of gold, and as having a "central headquarters." Actually, the meaning of the word "God," as we understand it and use it in the English language, is not found in the Aramaic text of the Bible. Our word "God" comes from the German language—a language Jesus never heard or spoke—and not from Aramaic, his native tongue. It is derived from the German word GOOT and means "The Good One." "God" doesn't express the full meaning and understanding of its Aramaic equivalent. There just isn't a corresponding word in English. The best one can do is simply to transliterate the Aramaic word—ALAHA (it is pronounced, ahl-*ah*-hah).

11

This Aramaic word for God, ALAHA, is also seen in the Arabic word, ALLAH, and in the Hebrew word, ALOHIM. (All three of these Semitic words come from the Aramaic root word AL.) The closest one may get to extracting a meaning from the word ALAHA, would be "Essence," "Substance," or "Premise." None of these words, by any means, should be taken as a definition for ALAHA. If one were to ask an Easterner what ALLAH means to him, he would not reply in theological terms, but in simple and direct language: "ALLAH is my *very breath,* and my *very heartbeat,* and my *very life.*" To the consciousness of the man of the Middle East, the living God encompasses him and watches over him as a shepherd watches over his flock. The words of the poetical psalmist describe this awareness very clearly:

O, Lord, You have searched me and known me. You know my downsitting and my uprising. You understand my thoughts from above. You know my way and my paths, and are acquainted with all my ways. For if there is deception in my tongue, lo, O Lord, You know it altogether. From the beginning to the end, You know me, O Lord, for You have formed and laid Your hand upon me. Such knowledge is too wonderful for me; it is high, I cannot attain to it. Where shall I go from your Spirit? or where shall I flee from your Presence? (Psalm 139:1-7)

12

Infinite Intelligence is Everywhere

Since ALAHA, or "God," is everywhere present and is the essence of all things, then we can easily see that we are living in a spiritual universe filled with God. The entire cosmic system is alive and dynamic. There is order in it all! There is intelligence in it all!

Let us take, for example, the tiny seed. It is a living chemical factory endowed with an intelligence all its own. The seed knows how to trap solar energy and convert it into itself. This secret man is trying to learn today. The seed also knows how to work with the law of death—to corrupt itself, to shed the old outer hull, and to release the new life. This little seed, then, will either give the world food to help sustain life, or it will help beautify our planet and make it a more livable place.

It is through our intelligence that we commune with the Living God. This intelligence within us is highly intuitive and sensitive. Our union with God is understood and felt intuitively, and *not just intellectually.* Inner Intelligence governs the physical body and regulates all the living cells that make life and health. "It is the Spirit that gives life" and thereby causes the body to grow. (See John 6:63) Our physical bodies are in the constant care of God, or Infinite Intelligence. This power continually and spontaneously works to heal all psychic and physical wounds we inflict upon ourselves, or which others inflict upon us.

Remember that the whole universe is filled with "God," for "God" is Spirit, and the Spirit means "that which is everywhere present." Therefore, the counsel and guidance we may need is there, ever-present for us to tap. But, what often happens is that we do not stay in tune to receive the guidance we need. Through negative mental attitudes, we tune into *other* channels, such as fear, worry, jealousy, and resentment. And sometimes we turn off our "receivers" altogether! So, we must consciously and actively "tune in" to God's guidance and counsel. After all, God is both *around* and *within* us, as the Scriptures clearly state. "For *in him* [God] we live and move and have our being." (Acts 17:28) ". . . To whom God wanted to make known the riches of the glory of this mystery among the Gentiles; which is Christ *in you*, the hope of glory." (Col.1:27) We can learn to work *with* God, through prayer. The Lord's Prayer teaches us the good and wholesome attitudes required for a state of communion or "tuning in."

A Misconception of Prayer

Prayer is not "telling God what to do." I believe He knows how to run His universe! Don't you agree? He doesn't have to be constantly reminded of our needs, nor of the needs of our relatives and friends. "And when you pray, do not repeat your words like the pagans, for they think that because of much talking they will be heard. Do not be like them, for your Father knows what you need, before you ask him." (Matt. 6:7-8) So, prayer is not "telling God," but it is listening to what God would tell us. *The purpose of prayer is not to change God, but to change us!* Do we really think that through prayer we may be able to move God to do something He wouldn't otherwise do? No prayer can make God more loving than He already is, or than He was in the past, or than He shall be in the future. No, what prayer accomplishes is this: it helps us to understand ourselves; it attunes us to spiritual forces around us and in us; and it helps us to understand our world and our fellow man.

We must also fully realize that we can *consciously* work with this inner intelligence to help us solve the problems we face in life. In fact, this is why Jesus gave us this method of prayer, or what I call, "attuning attitudes." There is only one Power in the universe, and through the goodness of this one Power, we can face our fears, which cause blockages, and overcome them. It takes courage, truthfulness, and freedom to face ourselves squarely; that is, to truly see our fears, hates, and resentments. But, by so doing, we will most naturally and spontaneously tune out the bad and tune in the good. Our minds and hearts are then, at that moment, free from fear, which limits and restricts the creative intelligence within us. Fear shuts the door to practical and sound living, but freedom opens the door of life for our good.

Jesus' understanding of prayer was one of direct and intimate communion with life forces—ALAHA. God is the essence of all life, both visible and invisible, both tangible and intangible. Prayer is our means of hearing the still small voice of our loving Father. And when we attune our minds with the proper attitude, then we can trap God's counsel, and thereby be "of one accord" with Him. (See John 10:30) This will enable us to live in harmony with His universal principles, instead of in opposition to them.

Praying "In Jesus' Name"

We are often instructed to pray "in Jesus' name." This statement is taken from Jesus' own directive, which is recorded in John 16:23-24:

Truly, truly, I say to you that whatever you ask my Father in my name, he will give it to you. Hitherto you have asked nothing in my name; ask and you will receive, so that your joy may be full.

16

Just what is the secret of praying "in Jesus' name"? Is it just uttering the name "Jesus" after each prayer? No, for the name "Jesus" was a very common name in Palestine. With so many men named "Jesus," there could be no magic in that particular name. Then what did Jesus mean when he said to pray "in his name"?

To truly pray "in his name" means to pray with the same kind of understanding about God and man that he had. The Aramaic word BESHEMI ("in my name") means "according to my technique, my way, my method, my approach, or my system of doing things," or "with my kind of understanding." Jesus encouraged his disciples to pray to the Father "in his name," but he meant for them to pray in the manner he taught them.

For example, scientists have learned the secret of splitting atoms through Einstein's method or formula. But they don't say, "In the name of Einstein, Atom, split!" And yet, many well-meaning people use Jesus' name in this very manner, and expect something magical to happen. Merely saying his name won't bring about the desired results any more than saying the name of Einstein will cause the atom to split of its own accord.

The answer to praying "in Jesus' name," then, lies in *experiencing* the same awareness that Jesus felt:

17

that God is a *loving Father;*
that *God* is *the* source of all good;
that man *gets* what he *expects,* and
that man *can* expect *good* things.

This is the spiritual equation that Jesus demonstrated and taught. Living in this kind of awareness negates all that is not good.

Practicing Jesus' Teachings

Jesus took a small group of simple young men from Galilee and taught them the secrets of prayer and God's Kingdom. Through these young men, Jesus changed the course of the world. He demonstrated to them what he meant by being "a son of God." He endowed them with spiritual insight and gifts to aid all humanity in transforming this world. His teachings enabled his disciples to overcome the problems created by a limited consciousness.

We, too, can learn to apply his teachings in our lives, and thereby live a more abundant life. There is nothing complicated or difficult about Jesus' method. The teaching of Jesus is simple, but we sometimes stumble at simplicity.

Jesus taught his disciples a new manner of praying because he knew some things they didn't understand. He knew that men did not have to beg and beseech God to give them the good things of life, as if He would not otherwise have done it. Jesus knew that all the good in the universe was already given for man's use. He knew that man's capacity to receive good is limited only by his failure to accept it and claim it. "If therefore you who err, know how to give good gifts to your sons, how much more will your Father in heaven give good things to those who ask him?" (Matt. 7:11)

Jesus opened the door for everyone to the Kingdom of Heaven when he told us that the Kingdom is "within you" or "among you." (See Luke 17:20-21) This means that the Kingdom is within your reach, but that you must act to lay hold of it.

"Quality" vs. "Quantity"

Jesus knew that man's spirit and God's Spirit are of the same essence, because he understood the divine revelation that declared man the very image and likeness of God. (See Gen. 1:26-27) This essence is the same in "quality" but, of course, not the same in "quantity." For example, a little spark of fire is of the same essence or "quality" as a great flame or a raging inferno, though not of the same "quantity."

God and man, then, being of the same spiritual essence, are able to commune—*the infinite with the*

Infinite. It is wonderful to realize that all men have the power to capture God's ideas, truth, and guidance. This equips man with all he needs to solve his problems and to grow. In fact, it is this unity with God that makes man's thought creative. It is this very creativity that enables man to continually be a co-worker with God. And it is by "tuning in" to Spirit that man learns to create only that which is good and worthwhile.

It is from this spiritual world of unseen realities that all discoveries and creative ideas come. All things visible have come from the realm of the invisible. And, since our minds are part of that invisible spiritual world, we are able to interpret and channel these unseen realities into our physical world of matter for the good of all. All these good gifts and enlightenment come from above; that is, from "our Father." "Every good and perfect gift is from above, and comes down from the Father of lights, with whom there is no variableness nor shadow of change." (James 1:17)

A Traditional Prayer

We are told that The Lord's Prayer was not totally original with Jesus. This prayer was prayed in the synagogues. Be that as it may, Jesus took this prayer and placed a different emphasis on various parts of it. He shifted the emphasis from a man-centered idea to a God-centered prayer. He changed certain words or attitudes, such as praying for the Kingdom of God, instead of praying for the political and nationalistic rule of Israel. We will discover more changes in the coming chapters.

A Mini-Gospel

The Lord's Prayer contains the essence of Jesus' entire teachings. It is a capsule summary of the message he preached for three-and-a-half years. It contains the message of the whole Bible. Even if we were to lose access to all of the Bible except The Lord's Prayer, we would still have the essence and meaning of religion.

Genuine Religion

Spiritual awareness is innate; it is an essential part of our beings. We must have order; we must have balance. And this is what "religion" means, in the Aramaic language. It comes from the Aramaic word DINA, which means "balance"—a balance in our own beings and a just, balanced relationship with others.

The Lord's Prayer, then, is a brief summary of Jesus' beliefs about God, mankind, and the world.

21

It is a synopsis of his understanding of the relationship between the material realm of the seen and the spiritual realm of the unseen.

Teach Us To Pray

Jesus' method of prayer is a simple and direct *acceptance* of the good the universe has for us. He knew that God, like a good father, is interested in the welfare and the well-being of His human family.

There is really no great secret of communing with God. But we must understand Jesus' concept of the Living God, and then let all other concepts which may be stumbling blocks and hindrances to us be removed.

The Lord's Prayer: A Translation

When Jesus' young disciples were with Him one day by the Lake of Galilee, they asked him to teach them to pray. Jesus immediately began to instruct them in his way of prayer. And he told them that when they prayed, they should pray in this manner:

Our Father who [is] throughout the universe,
Let your name be set apart.
Come your kingdom (counsel).
Let your desire be, as in the universe, also on the earth.

22

Give us bread for our necessities this day.

And free us from our offenses, as also we have freed our offenders.

And do not let us enter our temptation (worldliness), but set us free from error.

For belongs to you the kingdom, power, and song, from ages to ages.

Sealed in faithfulness.

—A literal translation from the Aramaic by the author

23

2

OUR UNIVERSAL FATHER

Jesus opened his prayer with the words AWOON DWASHMAYA: "Our Father who [is] in heaven." The phrase may also be translated, "Our Father who [is] in the universe," "Our Father who [is] everywhere," or just simply, "Our universal Father." Jesus comes right to the point, as he instructs his disciples to approach the Father directly, without intermediaries. With this opening statement, he immediately gave new meaning to this ancient prayer.

Prior to this time, when the people prayed, they didn't pray just to God. The petitioners' cries would be: "Oh, Father Abraham; Oh, Father Isaac; Oh, Father Jacob;" as if, for their forefathers' sake, but not their own, God would possibly hear them and grant their petitions. But Jesus made known to them, through his prayer, that God was their Father, and that He was interested in them for their own sake.

God was aware of all their needs. They did not need to approach Him through the Patriarchs. They didn't need *any* mediators. They could have direct communication with the Father Himself, for they, too, were just as important as the Patriarchs, in His sight!

Right away, we can see the lesson for us. We need no mediators or "go-betweens" when communing with God. *No one* in the past, in the present, or in the future has to be sought in order to talk with our Father. According to Jesus we don't need any priest, rabbi, minister, or guru to approach God. *We* are our own priests and our own intermediaries. Jesus revealed each man's individual relationship with God.

"Our Father" Is Approachable

In this entire marvelous prayer, Jesus nowhere mentions the word "God." He uses the Aramaic word ABA, "Father," or, as it appears here, AWOON, "Our Father." This gives us a sense of closeness. It is almost like saying "Dad" or "Papa." He taught his disciples that God is like a good father who is benevolent and kind. At that time, God was depicted as some mysterious, awesome, and fearsome deity who lived far from His creation. He would have nothing to do with the people. They had God so far removed from them that even His name was too holy to be spoken. But Jesus laid all this aside, for he taught his disciples that when they approached God, their attitude should be that of "Father."

In other words, "our heavenly Father" is approachable. We can always come to Him. But who can approach a God who is too far above us, too great, and too holy? He dwells in a light which no man can stand, as the Scriptures say in Exodus 33:20: "You cannot see my face; for no man can see me and live." We all quake and fear at this revelation. But Jesus changed this concept of God. He revealed the true nature of God. He is not someone to be feared. Rather, He is someone with whom anyone can commune. Jesus told them that God was like a good father who would lead, guide, and protect them. God desires good for everyone, and He can be approached by all without shame or hesitancy.

Sonship Now

And yet, we have been taught to approach God as if we were totally degraded, no good, unworthy sinners. *Jesus* never taught us this! It's a misunderstanding of Scripture! There were many people Jesus contacted who were good people and not "sinners." Jesus acknowledged the goodness in people when he gave the Beatitudes. (Matt. 5:1-12) He *didn't say*, "Blessed are the people who are *going to become* merciful," or "who are *going to become* pure in heart," or "who are *going to become* peacemakers." *He said*, "Blessed are the merciful;" "Blessed are the pure in heart;" "Blessed are the peacemakers." There are people who *are* merciful, who *are* pure in heart, and who *are* peacemakers. Jesus appealed to the good in people. Naturally, there were those who were going astray. But Jesus provided the means for them to be restored. No matter how far off the path some strayed, there was always a chance for reconciliation. Repentance and forgiveness were His way of restoration. (See Luke 24:46-47)

Approaching God as "Father" immediately puts us in intimate communion with Him. Prayer should not be an attempt to "get into" union with God. Prayer is the very acknowledgement of, and the very expression of, that union! It is because we *are* His sons that we can communicate with our Father. *At no time* can there be *separation* from God! If we believe that we are cut off or separated from Him, then it is we who bring the sense of division. It is not God who does this; it is our own mental attitude. God is! And He is everywhere! *He* hasn't changed! *We* have to change our wrong attitudes!

When we call God "Father," we are acknowledging our sonship with Him. We don't "work" our way into it; we just naturally have sonship because we are "His image and likeness." This opening phrase of The Lord's Prayer causes us to confess our

27

union with the eternal, living God, with the Father of all men.

Thus, the very first attitude we are to have, the first idea we are to "tune in to," is that we are one with our Father—now! All creation is in union with Infinite Intelligence. Once the truth of our sonship is truly accepted, we don't have to affirm it! Our children are our children, and they know it! We, too, must *settle* this matter, and once and for all, come to the full realization that *we are now God's sons!* (See I John 3:2)

Universal Presence

"Our Father" doesn't "condescend" to hear us or to be with us, because, like a human father, He enjoys being with His family. God doesn't have to *condescend,* nor do we have to *transcend,* to be in union with Him. These terms "condescend" and "transcend" have been misused in reference to the relationship between God and man. Of course, we can transcend our environment and problems, but what I am referring to is our relationship. God is Spirit; that is, that which is all-inclusive and everywhere. How can God "come down," or how can we "go up"? God is *in* us, *above* us, *around* us, *underneath* us, and *through* us. Jesus made this very clear to the Samaritan woman at the well (See John 4:21-24):

> Jesus said to her, Woman, believe me, the time is coming, when neither on this mountain nor in Jerusalem will they worship the Father. But the time is coming, and it is here, when the true worshippers shall worship the Father in spirit and in truth; for the Father also desires worshippers such as these. For God is Spirit; and those who worship him must worship him in spirit and in truth [that is, with understanding].

It's not just a "Deity" that is everywhere; it is the Presence of a fatherly Spirit that is everywhere. This Power is like a father giving good gifts, love, and aid to his children everywhere. The fatherly presence of God is in the very depths of our beings.

God can't be confined to any sacred shrine or contained in any one thing. No holy temple can house the universal Spirit of the living Father. Even King Solomon, after he had built the great and magnificent temple, prayed on its opening and dedication day: "Behold, heaven and the heaven of heavens cannot contain Thee; how much less this house which I have built?" (I Kings 8:27)

The great prophet Isaiah knew that Yahweh (Jehovah) was more than just a God to the Hebrews. He knew that He was the God of the whole universe, and that He couldn't be confined to any shrine or temple. Hear the words of Isaiah:

> Thus says the Lord: Heaven is my throne and the earth my footstool; what is the place that you build for me? And what is the place of my rest? For all those things has my own hand made, and all those things belong to me, says the Lord; and to whom shall I look, and where shall I dwell? But to him who is calm and humble, and trembles at my word. (Isa. 66:1-2)

All Races Are Sons

"Our universal Father" also means that God is the Father of all peoples and all races. He is not just "my" Father, or just "your" Father, or just "their" Father, but He is "our" Father. When we say the words, "*our* universal Father," we are automatically recognizing other peoples' sonship with the Father. God's Spirit fills the entire universe, and all things and all people exist in Him. This means that the Chinese, the Russians, the Japanese, the Arabs, and all peoples everywhere are sons of God!

God loves *all* His children! But when we pray, we often pray *only* for *our own* good, not caring about its effect on others. For instance, in warfare, we ask God to bless one side or the other. *God* cannot bless either side, for *He* doesn't participate in acts of aggression or violence. God acts only for the good of *all*! When we truly and deeply understand the meaning of *"our* universal Father," we *will* pray for *universal* good. We *will* empathize with *all* peoples and *act* for the good of *all*.

The First Attunement

Through his teaching, Jesus freed man from the limiting and mistaken concept of a sectarian, nationalistic, partisan God. Spirit, or "God," is like pure water which flows freely everywhere, watering the dry ground and quenching the thirst of all men. All men must have water and air in order to live. Pure water and air are the same everywhere. And so is our Father. This is our Savior's concept of the living God, Whom he called "Father," and Whom he taught us to acknowledge as "our Father."

Thus, the opening statement of The Lord's Prayer causes us to confess our union with God, and with our fellowmen, who are all His children. This is God's way! This is "our universal Father"! What a positive way to begin prayer! This is our first attunement.

Aramaic Old Testament manuscript—464 A.D. (British museum)   A portion of Genesis, chapter 41

°°

3

HALLOWED BE
THY NAME

NITHKADASH SHMAKH means "Holy be thy name." It may also be translated, "Let your name be set apart." The word KADISH, "holy," means "to be set aside for a specific purpose," "dedicated," "distinct," or "separate." For example, if I said to you, "Please set that glass aside for me for the lecture this evening," then the drinking glass would become "holy"; that is, "set aside for a specific function." It would not be used for any other purpose until the time I was to give the talk. It was because men were using God's name *falsely* that Jesus reminded his disciples (and us) to keep God's name apart from *wrong* deeds and transactions.

False Oaths

In the East, when businessmen sold articles, they would call upon God's name in their bargaining. They would raise a hand to the heavens and swear in God's name, taking an oath like this: "In the name of God (ALLAH) and all His holy messengers, this shirt is worth $10.00, but you may have it for only $5.00." Many times bargaining would last for hours, using God's name, the names of the saints, and even members of the household. All this was done to bolster their sales pitch. And then, if the merchant should fail to sell his article, he would become angry, swear, and spit. This use of God's name in everyday business was unnecessary, according to Jesus. The sellers dragged God's name down into lying oaths and misleading conversations.

Jesus was against the use of God's name in false oaths, as seen in his comment recorded in Matthew 5:37: "But let your words be yes, yes, and no, no; for anything which adds to these is a deception." If one should call on God's name in an oath, then he should speak the plain, straight truth!

Jesus' authority for this teaching was the third commandment, found in Exodus 20:7. It has been translated: "Thou shalt not take the name of the Lord thy God *in vain.*" The term "in vain" is not correct. The Aramaic word is DAGALOOTHA, "in falsehood." Thus, a more accurate rendering would be: "You shall not take the name of the Lord your God in falsehood or falsely." In other words, God's name should be kept apart from *lying* words and *false* oaths.

Other Wrong Uses

Men have also used God's name wrongly in many other ways. In His name, they have carried on wars, persecutions, crusades, and massacres. Men have killed in their fanatical zeal, thinking that they were doing God a great favor. It was considered a divine virtue to kill those of an opposing religion or faith. False teachers and false prophets have taught evil and erroneous doctrines, in His name, to suit their own desires, and have thereby destroyed the souls and minds of men.

The Second Attunement

God is holy; that is, He is apart from all error and evil. But His holiness doesn't mean that He is unapproachable or distant and aloof. Many have a mistaken idea about God's holiness. Humanly speaking, God is dedicated to the good of all humanity, for, after all, He created us in "His image and likeness."

The idea of God's holiness should remind us that He takes no part in evil transactions or in deeds which hurt, destroy, or kill people. This is why Jesus told his disciples to pray, "Hallowed [or holy] be thy name." Let us keep our Father's name holy—separate from error and falsehood—for God has no part in untruth. God's name represents all that is good. So let us speak God's name in goodness and truth only. All good surrounds His name. This is our second attunement.

4

THY KINGDOM COME

TAYTHEY MALCOOTHAKH means, "Come your kingdom." There is no doubt about it! Jesus, in his inner being, had transcended all racial, religious, and nationalistic boundaries! He foresaw a world without the selfishness of individual rivalry. But most of his people were still looking for an earthly, partisan kingdom. They were eagerly yearning for and expecting the long-overdue restoration of the Davidic Kingdom. They wanted the Romans defeated, Herod dethroned, and the rule of Israel established again. The prayers of the people were constantly directed to this end and for this kind of kingdom.

A Spiritual Kingdom

But, once again, Jesus shifted the emphasis of the traditional prayer. He taught his disciples that they should pray for God's Kingdom, a spiritual kingdom that rules from inside the hearts of men, instead of a political materialistic kingdom, that is imposed upon men from the outside. He knew that men's kingdoms alone would always bring strife and problems, but that God's Kingdom embraces all nations and peoples impartially. He knew that in God's Kingdom, true justice prevails for all, because one equal measure—the measure of love—is used for all nations and peoples.

Counsel and Advice

MALCOOTHA, "kingdom," also means "counsel" and "advice." It comes from the same root as the words "angel," "king," and "counselor." God's Kingdom is a state in which God's guidance is carried out. In it, the "inner man" rules, not with force and regulations, but with divine counsel and loving-kindness. Thus, when we pray for "God's Kingdom" to come, we are actually praying, "Let God's counsel or advice come into our lives to guide and direct us rightly."

Our Kingdoms vs. God's Kingdom

God's counsel will always guide us away from trouble, if we consult Him and heed His counsel.

39

The reason for the difficulties the world is experiencing today is that God's counsel and advice are not being sought. Actually, man inwardly knows the truth of God's guidance, but he doesn't act upon it. God's Kingdom is universal and upholds justice and equality for all. But we're always looking one way only, and that is, looking out just for ourselves and how best we will be benefitted. We usually pray only for *our* nation and for *our* way. Yet, when we say, "Come your kingdom (counsel)," we're actually asking for God's counsel to be revealed to us so we can carry it out in our lives. His counsel is just and balanced. It's not a long measure for this person, and a short measure for that person. The measure is the same for all. When God's guidance comes, it is fair and just. When man's counsel comes, it is one-sided. Someone's going to get cheated somewhere. But God's counsel is always fair for all concerned.

The Kingdom *Within*

Through this part of his prayer, Jesus is again teaching us to raise our sights, to see a greater kingdom than man's, and to tune in to the advice of God that will bring about His Kingdom in us and among men.

When asked by the Pharisees about the coming of God's Kingdom, Jesus told them: "The kingdom of God does not come by observation. Neither will they say, Behold, it is here! or, behold, it is there! for behold, the kingdom of God is within [among] you." (Luke 17:20-21)

This means that God's Kingdom is not somewhere far off, but that it is within our reach. And it also means that it is up to us to demonstrate it in our own lives! It is not something that will be thrust on us from the outside, overwhelming all in its way, and giving no opportunity for choice. We won't wake up some morning and discover that the Kingdom of God was established overnight. The Kingdom will be established *only* as each of us *sees* the truth and *acts* upon it!

God's Kingdom *First*

Jesus also said, "Seek first the kingdom of God and His righteousness, and all these things shall be added to you." (Matt. 6:33) To "seek God's Kingdom first" means to open our minds and hearts to God's guidance, above all else. When we do this, then we are guided so that all of our needs, material and otherwise, can flow to us, and out from us again. God's guidance will always lead us into paths of blessing. It will enable us to solve all our problems, both individually and nationally, when we truly see it and act upon it. When this is done, then we need

41

not be anxiously concerned about "our" way, for we will be seeking the best way for all, and "all" includes us, too.

The Third Attunement

Will we turn to, and act upon, God's counsel? Will we take the steps necessary to look beyond just our own interests, and see a larger world of peace and harmony for all peoples? When we truly pray in this manner, our prayers and thoughts become universal; we truly want good to be manifested for all.

We already do many things which are right and good, and we already have many attitudes which are wholesome. That is God working through us. In Philippians 2:13, we read: "for it is God who inspires you with the will to do the good things which you desire to do."

Let us open ourselves fully to God's counsel, and live our lives within its wisdom. Then we will be living a life that will *naturally* produce peace and harmony. The Kingdom, the guidance, begins *within*. It's our choice! This is our third attunement.

5

LET YOUR WISH BE

The Aramaic words NEHWEH SEVIANAKH
AICANNA DWASHMAYA OP BARAH mean "thy will
be done, as in heaven so on earth." Literally translated, they mean, "let your wish be, as in the universe, also on the earth." The Aramaic word SE-
VIANAKH means "thy will," "thy desire," "thy
wish," "thy delight," or "thy pleasure."

The Will of God

The term "the will of God" should be properly
understood as "God's good desire for His children."
Very often the will of God is thought of as something
mystifying, elusive, sanctimonious, or unpleasant. It
is thought of as something contrary to our own will.
We also equate the word "will" with the word "force."
But the use of the word SEVIANA in The Lord's

Prayer does not imply that God is going to impose something distasteful on us.

No Cause For Dismay

What, then, is the will of God? How often have I been asked this question. And how many times in my many years as a pastor did I counsel people who were struggling "to know God's will" for their lives. How many people have been burdened with guilt because they felt they were not doing "the will of God." Such frustration people suffer trying to discover God's will! Just what is Jesus revealing in this phrase of his prayer?

First of all, let us return for a moment to Jesus' original thought—our Father—not "God Almighty." He is talking about our Father's will or wish, not the will of an awesome, demanding Deity!

What kind of Father would God be if He made it difficult for us to learn or to know His will? And if He does, indeed, have a "will" for us, then surely He, above all others, would want us to know His will.

What Is God's Wish?

Let's remember that this is not "God Almighty" with Whom we are communing, but it is "our Father." And what does a father wish for his children?

What do you wish for your children? What do I wish for my children? Don't we wish for them to get along; that they will be healthy and prosperous; that they will have peace of mind; that they will understand and be able to relate to others; that they will find peace and harmony, not only among themselves, as brothers and sisters, but also in their relationships with others; and that they will have the wisdom and the maturity to journey safely on this planet?

Isn't this what we desire for our children? Don't we desire good things for them? Why do we, then, complicate the matter of God's will? Jesus explained it so clearly: "If therefore you who err, know how to give good gifts to your sons, how much more will your Father in heaven give good things to those who ask him?" (Matt. 7:11) If we know how to give good gifts to our children, and we make mistakes, how much more, then, must our heavenly Father, Who has bestowed this intelligence upon us, wish for us to be in health, to prosper, to have understanding, to have peace and harmony? This is "the will of God" for us! This is God's desire for us!

We don't have to beg our Father to find out what His will is! He's a Father. He wants us to live, and to live freely and happily. It's that simple. Truth is never complicated nor difficult. And neither is our Father's wish complicated or difficult to understand.

God Doesn't Inflict Suffering

We have been taught that it is "the will of God" for us to suffer! For example, when we are sick, we may even question our "right" to get well. Or we may believe that God wants us to be sick so that He may teach us compassion and empathy. But this is not God's way of teaching us compassion and empathy. However, because we haven't rightly understood "our Father's will," we may have resigned ourselves to a life of poverty, illness, loneliness, and suffering.

When our children become sick, don't we do everything in our power to make them well? I'm sure we wouldn't inflict suffering on our children to teach them a lesson! We want our children to learn and to be sensitive and empathetic, but we don't want them to be ill to learn this lesson. If we who make mistakes know how to give good gifts to our children, how much more does our heavenly Father! No, our Father does not send us sickness to teach us a lesson. We bring misfortune upon our own heads without the help of God. Hopefully, though, when our suffering hurts badly enough, we will wake up to the error of our ways, and change the causes which brought on our troubles.

God doesn't inflict any evil upon people! Diseases, for example, are brought about by our breaking natural health laws. We are often insensitive to our bodily needs. We also violate the laws of a healthy mind; and hatred, resentment, and bitterness show up in our bodies as various forms of illnesses. Sicknesses are also caused by the environment and certain cultural patterns. I say these things merely to show that it is not God Who causes these evils. We have "created" these problems by going against our own good, either through ignorance or deliberately. Disease does not originate with God. When we realize that God is *for* us, then who or what can be against us? (See Rom. 8:31)

Universal Harmony

SHMAYA means "sky," "heaven," "cosmos," or "universe." Metaphorically, it means "prosperity," "peace," and "harmony." The ancient savants and prophets used the term "heaven" to indicate "a universal state of peace and harmony" and also "a personal consciousness of peace and harmony." They used the idea of "the heavens" because they'd observed how the planets and other heavenly bodies stayed in their orbits. We also realize how harmoniously the heavenly bodies function.

Through the centuries, mankind has gradually learned why this is so. We have discovered that there are natural and unchangeable laws built into the elements of the physical universe which cause them to act in definite and harmonious ways. By merely being just what they are, the elements of the universe express these inner laws, and thereby "live together" in balance and in peace. The very essence of the universe is order and intelligence.

"Religion" Means "Balance"

As stated earlier, the Aramaic word for religion is DINA, meaning "balance." Just as each planet or star in the universe is dependent upon other heavenly bodies, so we, too, are interdependent and interrelated with one another. Remove the balance and order from the universe, and we will have chaos. The same thing happens to us when there is no order, intelligence, or balance functioning in our society.

The Intelligence which we call "God" is that cohesive force which keeps everything in balance. Religion is the study of God and of the balance which results from the operation of His laws. Thus, religion should teach us to keep a just, balanced relationship within ourselves and with others.

"Do Ye Likewise"

Jesus is giving us an example of how God's wish should be carried out on the earth—just as it is carried out in the heavens; that is, by working with, instead of fighting against, the built-in laws of our being, which are God-given inclinations to do good. Jesus is teaching us that we must be sensitive to the spiritual forces which are within us if we would have peace. Just as the elements of the universe obey their innate laws, so must we, too, cooperate with our innate spiritual powers. In this way, we will live together in peace and harmony.

The natural laws of the universe are designed for flawless operation. But when man decides to break the laws of his being, he moves out of his orbit. And what happens when we move out of orbit? We collide and harm one another, and everyone suffers. But by understanding ourselves and by working with the laws of our being, we can avoid collisions and much unnecessary suffering.

The Fourth Attunement

Our Lord is teaching us to "tune in" to God, to align ourselves with the harmony which prevails throughout the universe. When we say these words in sincerity, we are admitting that we desire God's wish to be done on the earth just as faithfully as it is done in the heavens. By awakening this attitude, we are opening our consciousness to the possibility of universal peace on the earth; that is, perfect harmony among all the parts. We are preparing ourselves to receive the good which our loving Father is giving to us.

Thus, when we pray these words we are confessing that we want to stay in our own orbits, that we want to be our "real" selves, and not collide with ourselves or with each other. We are affirming with all our heart that we will work with our intrinsic powers, so that the same harmony, beauty, and oneness which we see expressed in the universe may also flow among mankind. By so attuning ourselves, we will express these divine forces which are within us. We will feel and radiate truth and life to all. This is the fourth attunement.

6

GIVE US BREAD TODAY

HAVLAN LAKHMA DSONKANAN YOMANA means "Give us bread for our necessities today." In the East, people live more simply than we do here in the West. They are content with the provision which comes each day. For example, Eastern women don't make up a supply of bread to last for several days. Instead, they bake their bread every day for that day's needs alone. And not only do they bake enough for their own family's needs, but they also bake extra bread for the needs of travelers who might happen to stop, seeking food for their journey. Easterners are hospitable to travelers whenever they stop, be it day or night. They know that the stranger they feed today may be their own host tomorrow, so they treat each other, and even their enemies, helpfully.

Eastern Bread

When you think of this Eastern bread, however, don't picture a "loaf" of bread, as we have here today. The bread of the Eastern people is like a Mexican tortilla—thin, very flat, and round. But it's not small! You can hold a tortilla in your hand, but Eastern bread is large. Once, when in the Holy Land, we fed about 40 people with one of these "loaves."

This bread can be folded like a handkerchief and carried in a pocket. And this is just what is done in the East when people journey. Because inns are scarce and unpredictable, Easterners must take their food with them for the entire trip. And it is their custom, when they sit down to eat, to share their food with anyone else present. So, when on a journey and their food supply is running short, they simply eat as they walk along, carefully pulling the food out of their robes so it won't be seen by others, and so they won't be obliged to share their limited and dwindling supply. This is why the Bible speaks of "bread eaten in secret" as being "pleasant." (See Proverbs 9:17) But this proverb also has another connotation, which Dr. Lamsa explains in his *Old Testament Light* commentary.

Spiritual Bread

The term LAKHMA, "bread," doesn't mean just food or material things alone, however. It also means "understanding" and "truth." Jesus even spoke of himself as "the Bread of Life." His Truth gives us an understanding of life, and of God, and of ourselves and our fellow men. God has truly given us "bread from heaven," as well as understanding, to meet our needs from day to day.

When Jesus was out in the desert wrestling with negative forces, he repudiated the first temptation with the words of Moses. Hear his words, as recorded in Matthew 4:4:

> It is written that it is not by bread alone that man can live, but by every word which proceeds from the mouth of God.

The words, as first spoken by Moses, are recorded in Deut. 8:3:

> . . . man does not live by bread alone; but by everything that proceeds out of the mouth of the Lord does man live.

Moses was telling us that material things alone cannot satisfy. We must live by the words of truth and guidance which come from God. If we do, our heavenly Father will surely guide us to the appropriate channels of His supply to provide us with the material things we need, for then we will be working in accord with the law of supply.

But, more importantly, Moses was telling us that material wealth alone will not bring equality, justice, and social order. He understood that having abundant wealth, without having the word that proceeds from God's mouth—Truth and Justice—would only lead to violence, chaos, and a disintegrating world. If we would have order in the world, we must first have order within. And inner harmony comes only by Love and Truth.

> And one of them who knew the law, asked him, testing him, Teacher, which is the greatest commandment in the law?
> Jesus said to him, Love the Lord your God with all your heart and with all your soul and with all your might and with all your mind.
> This is the greatest and the first commandment.
> And the second is like to it, Love your neighbor as yourself.
> On these two commandments hang the law and the prophets. (Matt. 22:35-40)

"All These Things"

We do need material things. But when we think only of material things and neglect our spiritual development, we lose our way. We strive, in erroneous and harmful ways, to obtain the things we need. In such cases, it is not the things themselves which are wrong, but the way in which we obtain them. However, by maintaining our spiritual focus and a system of values based on spiritual understanding, we will be led to obtain, in good and right ways, the things we need. This is what Jesus meant when he taught us to:

Seek first the kingdom of God and his righteousness, and all these things shall be added to you. (Matt. 6:33)

Our universal Father knows the things we need, and He supplies all our needs. He is "the Supply," while all other sources are only channels through which His inexhaustible supply flows. And He provides daily, as we have need.

Nature Always Provides

According to the account of creation given in the first chapter of Genesis, man did not come on the scene until the sixth day of creation, and he was well provided for when he did arrive. Food, shelter, and the basic needs of life were all created first, in preparation for him. The earth was then ready to take care of him. Nature always provides for its many species, but each species must look for and appropriate for its use nature's generous provision. However, man often thinks he needs more than nature provides, or that there isn't enough to go around. And his greed and unnecessary, excessive accumulation of wealth for tomorrow have brought about an imbalance in our world.

Wealth

Wealth is good for all when it is circulated and properly shared. But there must be proper circulation in order to maintain it. Wealth must be circulated, and not just accumulated, if it is to grow. When we start hoarding things, we lose them. By hoarding, we are blocking the flow of good *from* us *and to* us. And our fear of lack sets up a "lack vibration" which attracts to us the very thing we fear. Circulation is the positive action which keeps good flowing to all people, including ourselves.

The Fifth Attunement

God has always provided for man. James 1:17 tells us:

> Every good and perfect gift is from above, and comes down from the Father of lights, with whom there is no variableness nor shadow of change.

The Father has given man the intelligence and the understanding to discover new and hidden resources for the betterment of mankind. All that man needs has already been provided for him. But he needs spiritual guidance to bring it about properly, with good to all and harm to none. With this kind of understanding, we can know that our needs will be met daily, for we are tuned in to the Source of all good, and our Supply will not fail us. This is the fifth attunement.

Word-for-word breakdown and phonetic pronunciation guide to the Lord's Prayer

English Translation	Aramaic Pronunciation	Original Aramaic
Our Father	Ä-WOŎN	
who (is) in heaven	D'WÄSH-MĀYÄ	
holy be	NĬTH-KĂ-DĂSH	
your name	SHMÄKH	
let come	TĀY-THĀY	
your kingdom	MĂL-COÖ-THÄKH	
let be	NĒWĀY	
your desire (will)	SĒV-YÄ-NÄKH	
even as in	ÄI-KĔN-NÄ	
heaven	D'WÄSH-MĀYÄ	
so on earth	ŎP-BÄRÄH	
give us	HÄW-LĂN	
bread	LÄKH-MÄ	
for our needs	D'SOÖN-KÄ-NÄN	
from day to day	YAW-MÄ-NÄ	
forgive us	WÄSH-WŌK-LĂN	

our offenses	KHŌ-BĀĬN
even as	ÄI-KĔN-NÄ
we also have	DÄP-KHÄ-NÄN
forgiven	SH-WÄK-ĔN
our offenders	ĔL-KHÄ-YÄ-UĔN
and let not	OÖ-LÄ
us enter	TÄ-LÄN
into temptation	ĔL-NIS-YŌ-NÄ
but	ĔL-LÄ
part us	PÄ-SÄN
from (error) evil	MĔN BEE-SHÄ
because	MĬT-THŌL
yours	D'LÄKH
are	HEE
kingdom	MÄL-COÖ-THÄ
and power	OÖ-KHÄY-LÄ
and glory (song)	OÖ-TĬSH-BŌKH-TÄ
from ages	ĔL-ÄL-ÄM
through ages	ÄL-MEEN
sealed in trust, faith, and truth	Ä-MĔN

59

7

FREE US
FROM OUR OFFENSES

WASHBOKLAN KHOBEN: AICANNA DOP KHNAN SHBAKN LKHAYAVEN means "Forgive us our offenses, as we have forgiven our offenders." A literal translation would read: "Free us [from] our offenses as also we have freed our offenders." The word KHOBEN used here means something more than just "debts," as it has been translated in other translations of the Bible. It also means "faults," "mistakes," or "offenses." And the word SHBAKN which has been translated as "forgive," also means "to free," "to untie," "to loosen," or "to release."

Forgiveness Frees Us

Forgiveness frees us from past errors which we have committed, or which have been committed against us, and enables us to start on a new path of life. Genuine forgiveness heals any hurts or wrongs. It strengthens the disheartened soul which has lost its way. It refreshes and renews our hope. It is through forgiveness that we are "born again" and "become like a child." In this way we regain the precious attitude of a willing mind which is ready to learn all over again.

Nature Doesn't Condemn

Jesus was a strong advocate of forgiveness. This is one of the important teachings which makes his Gospel so appealing and so powerful. He knew, through his own experiences of life and through his study of the Scriptures, that Nature does not blame nor "point its finger" when things go wrong. Nature always endeavors to heal or correct an injury or hurt. For example, when I cut my finger, the life forces in my body immediately rush to the aid of the injured area to fight off infection and to start the coagulation of the blood to prevent excessive bleeding. The body doesn't attempt to seek out the one who did the damage. Its only interest is to repair the wound.

Jesus knew that God is a loving, forgiving Father Who cares for His children. He also knew that forgiveness is the beginning of the rectification of all human mistakes. Blaming doesn't heal anything, but forgiveness does. Our Lord, understanding mankind as he did, made room for human weaknesses and faults and stressed the need for practicing forgiveness. He knew that forgiveness would restore broken human relationships.

A Two-Way Street

"And free us from our offenses." How we all love this part of the prayer, for we all long to be free of the guilt which accompanies past offenses. But there's a catch to it: "as also we have freed our offenders." How often we seem to overlook this important part! We all want to be freed from our offenses. We also want other people to put up with our shortcomings. But how well do we put up with their shortcomings? In other words, through these words of the prayer we are asking: "Let me experience the same freedom from my offenses as I have allowed others to experience." Let us stop and think about that for a moment. How many times I have heard people say, "I forgive him," and then a few minutes later they start talking about him again. They haven't released the offense. They're still holding onto it!

When we hold grudges and allow them to build up in our minds, we suffer mentally and physically. We often become unbearable to live with. When we don't forgive others, how can we expect forgiveness to be extended to us? If we become difficult and unforgiving toward others, they will treat us likewise. It is impossible to escape the law of reaping what we have sown. We find that what we really think of ourselves, deep within, is felt by others and reflected back to us as their "impression" of us. It is essential, for our sake and theirs, that we learn to forgive others and to forgive ourselves as well. It is also interesting to realize that we always keep the "original copy" of whatever we send out to others, be it hate and resentment, or love and forgiveness.

"Wise as Serpents"

This does not mean, however, that we should not be careful of certain people who are determined to do evil. Jesus told his disciples to be "wise as serpents." (See Matt. 10:16) He used this example because he 'had observed that when a serpent sees trouble coming it gets out of the way; it wants to avoid being stepped on. And we should do this also! When we see trouble coming we should get out of its way, side-step it.

Thus, be wise when you know a person does evil and wishes to hurt. You can forgive him, but stay out of his way lest you get "stepped on." Therefore, be "wise as serpents."

"Pure as Doves"

In the passage just mentioned, Jesus also told his disciples to be "pure as doves." Doves love to go where people are gentle, where people are good. They love to sit on the shoulder of a meek man. They make their nests in certain homes because they know they will not be mistreated there. They sense it, and the people love to have them nearby.

There's a reference to this phenomenon in the Song of Solomon 2:12:

> The flowers appear on the earth; the time of pruning has come, and the voice of the turtle dove is heard in our land;

In most English translations "turtle dove" has been wrongly translated as "turtle." This is very misleading, since the "voice" of the turtle cannot be heard. The voice of the turtle dove, however, is a joy to all; hearing it means the doves have built a nest nearby and there is tranquility and peace. When people are upset and there is quarreling in the homes, the doves leave. They become frightened at the vibrations they feel from the trouble in the homes, but when they stay it is a sign of peace and harmony.

If we are to be "pure as doves," then we must have a forgiving but wise heart. We shouldn't remain where there is constant strife or where there are troublemakers. We must be at peace with all and avoid trouble whenever possible.

Self-Forgiveness, Too

But there is something more to consider about forgiveness. Jesus was teaching us here that our own forgiveness comes to us through the act of practicing forgiveness. If we don't forgive others, it's hard for us to forgive ourselves. People who refuse to forgive others usually won't forgive themselves either. But when a person releases others he usually will not hold a grudge against himself.

"Pure in Heart"

These words of the prayer help us to tune in to the needs of others and to our own needs. They help us to clear our minds of hatred and resentment so we may again commune with one another and with our Father. They help us to purify our minds, for, as Jesus said, "Blessed are the pure in heart [those who have a clear mind and conscience], for they shall see God." (Matt. 5:8)

The Sixth Attunement

Forgiveness revitalizes our souls and releases the inner tensions and bondages which plague our minds. This attunement would not be complete without the powerful act of forgiveness for ourselves and for others. This is the sixth attunement.

8
DO NOT LET US ENTER INTO WORLDLINESS

OOLA TALAN LNISUNA ELLA PASAN MIN BISHA: "And do not let us enter into temptation, but deliver us from evil." Most other translations of this verse read like this: "And do not *lead us* into temptation. . . ." But the correct translation from the Aramaic reads: "And do not let us enter into temptation. . . ."

It's interesting to note that Benjamin Franklin, like many others, was perplexed by the King James version of The Lord's Prayer. So he "modernized" it. His version of this particular phrase read: "And keep us out of temptation." Without knowing Aramaic, he was very close to the original meaning; it was certainly an improvement over asking God not to lead us into temptation!

God never leads anyone into temptation, nor does he tempt anyone! God is light, life, and love. How could He lead us into temptation? How could light lead us into darkness? The fact is that light always overcomes darkness, but darkness cannot overcome light. And love does not tempt us to do evil.

How would we feel if our children continually asked us, "Dad, Mom, don't lead us into temptation." No, our children know that we want to lead them away from trouble and temptation. And the same is true of our heavenly Father.

When we are led into temptation, it is by our own desire, as the Apostle James tells us in his epistle:

> Let no man say when he is tempted, I am tempted of God; for God cannot be tempted with evil, neither does he tempt any man;
> But every man is tempted by his own lust; he covets and is enticed. (James 1:13-14)

The Aramaic word TALAN comes from the root word AL, which has many connotations. Among these are "to enter into," "to attack," and "to wrestle." And when used as a preposition, it means "on," "upon," "in," "by," "alongside of," or "on top of."

In this phrase of the prayer, however, it means "do not let us enter." The same word is used by

Jesus in Matthew 26:41, when he said to his apostles: "Awake and pray, that you may not enter (TALON) into temptation."

"Materialism"

The Aramaic word NISUNA means "trials," and "temptation." Another connotation or nuance would be materialism or worldliness. Temptations and trials come from materialism or worldliness. "Do not let us enter into materialism." In other words, we are asking here, "Do not let us be deceived by the materialistic way of life." This does not mean that we are to avoid using material things. Rather, we are not to lose ourselves in them.

Nevertheless, materialism often dominates our thinking. Because of this, we lose sight of the spiritual principles which bring about the material effects we see. When we see only the effect (materialism), and not the cause (the spiritual principle of supply), we have lost our balance. Through this phrase of the prayer, then, we are asking to keep a balance between spiritual principle and material things.

"Part Us"

The Aramaic word PASAN means "part us" or "separate us," or "set us free" and not just "deliver us." The word "deliver" does not carry the full impact of the original word. We don't want just to be "delivered" once we're involved in a situation. We want to be "parted" or "separated" from trouble before we become ensnared by it. We want to avoid trouble by being guided away from it ahead of time.

"Evil" or "Mistakes"?

The word BISHA, usually translated as "evil," has many meanings in Aramaic. For instance, it means "bad," "mistake," "error," "immature," and "unripe." But in this verse it means "error" or "mistake."

We can get a clearer understanding of this word by recalling a story from the prophet Jeremiah. In Jeremiah, chapter 24, there is a discussion about a basket of "very good" figs and a basket of "very bad" or "evil" figs. We might wonder what the figs ever did to be "evil." They did nothing! The word used here simply means that they were unripe. In the East, when people bite into a fruit which is sour, they say, for example, "This is an 'evil' fig," because it's unripe. So the word BISHA, used here, simply means "mistakes."

It does not refer to "the evil one," as we find in some Bible translations. However, if one chooses to interpret it as "the evil one," it would simply mean "an evil person," that is, a liar, a thief, or anyone who would mislead or harm us. It would not mean "a supernatural being." There is only one Power in the universe, and that is ALAHA (God). It is we who create our problems—from our wrong choices, our ignorance, our misunderstandings, our immaturity, and from our misleading philosophies and ideologies.

Only God Can "Part Us" From Mistakes

Only God—the true, good, inherent spiritual Power Who is a living part of us all—can direct us and separate us from evil or mistakes. When we depend on God, and not only on what our eyes see, or on our physical desires alone, we will be able to avoid many situations which ordinarily would overtake us. Material things are necessary, but they should never become our ultimate goal. If this happens, we are blinded spiritually, and we take dangerous shortcuts which inevitably lead us into trouble.

God's Spirit will always enable us to see the right way, if we will heed His inner guidance. And if we do make a mistake, He will guide us in our restoration. We can learn from our mistakes and then go on to new and better ways.

The Seventh Attunement

The thought being expressed in this part of the prayer is, "Do not let us enter into, become ensnared by, or become saturated with, materialism, but, as we make our gains, part us from mistakes which hurt ourselves or others." Yes, we are to make gains, and our needs are to be met. But it should always be done with the idea of circulation, and not just accumulation, since the balance of the entire universe depends on the circulation of the good which Nature provides.

When we pray this phrase of the prayer, we awaken and call upon our inner spiritual forces, so we may be guided by them, and not misled by outward material things. We are opening ourselves to God's counsel. By doing so, we can avoid many mistakes and bring greater happiness to ourselves and to others. This is the seventh attunement.

9
BELONGS TO YOU KINGDOM, POWER, AND GLORY

MITTOL DILAKHYE MALCOTHA OKHELA OOTISHBOKHTA: LALAM ALMIN AMEN means, "For thine is the kingdom and the power and the glory for ever and ever. Amen." A literal translation would be, "For belongs to You kingdom, power, and glory, from ages to ages. Amen. (Sealed in faithfulness.)" Again, it may also be translated, "Yours is the kingdom, power, and song throughout all the ages."

Now Comes His Majesty

Jesus now brings in the majesty and power of our Father, not at the beginning of the prayer, but at the end. His approach at the beginning is "our Father" or "Papa"—a loving, compassionate, approachable Father, and not a far-off, unapproachable Potentate. This is how we are to approach God—with a sense of oneness and relationship.

Now, at the end of the prayer, he acknowledges the Source of the power we need to carry out the truth expressed in this prayer—the One Who makes possible the attunements which we have affirmed. "For belongs to You kingdom, power, and glory." Through these words, we are expressing something like this: "Dad, I know you can do it, because you've got it all! Yours is the kingdom; Yours is the advice, the counsel, the power, the glory; the magnificence: it is Yours! You have what it takes to provide for our needs." When our children come to us and ask us for things, they ask because they know we will do our best to provide their needs. How much more so will "our heavenly Father" provide for us when we ask Him!

The Eternal Kingdom

The Aramaic words LALAM ALMIN mean, "from ages to ages." Many people say "world without end," but that doesn't quite convey the meaning expressed in the Aramaic words Jesus used. He was teaching us that the kingdom or counsel of God always remains faithful and unchanging "from ages to ages."

We often think that one person or one nation has "the answer" for the world, but that's not the case, as history has proven. At one time Assyria ruled the world. Then Babylon ruled, and later Persia, Greece, and Rome. The Saracens then ruled the world, and they were replaced by the Ottoman Empire. Then the British Commonwealth spread its wings over the world. Today other great nations are in power. Nevertheless, "the kingdom" is always in God's hands.

All nations rise and fall. No human kingdom survives from ages to ages, from everlasting to everlasting. Only one kingdom endures from everlasting to everlasting—God's universal kingdom. This is why we say "thine is the kingdom" which endures "from ages to ages." God doesn't change. He is the same from ages to ages. It is we who awaken to Him!

The Universal Kingdom

If we would only give glory to God, instead of aspiring just to our own glory, then we wouldn't battle over boundaries or strive for world domination. We would realize that our Father wants good for all His children. To Him no one nation is greater or better than another. We would realize that His guidance is equal for all nations.

Whether we speak of a nation or of an individual, each is unique and each contributes to life in his own particular way. Every race and every people contribute something of value to the whole of mankind. This is because all good things come, finally, from our Father's counsel and guidance, in the form of ideas. It is through our Father's universal Counsel—His kingdom, His power, and His glory—that good for everyone will be accomplished.

Science and Religion

We may think that because we have advanced in technology we have also advanced in religion. But we have not. We have gone backward, instead of forward, for we have lost much of the true sense of the science of religion. We're accomplishing much with technology, but little in the field of religion. Even Jesus' teachings are not fully nor properly understood after all this time. And we have often failed to implement those teachings we have understood well. We have become too bogged down in outward forms and dogmas and have set aside his original teachings. But now, we can return to this truth, expressed so simply so long ago by the Master. We will make progress in religion as more and more people open their minds to his guidance and counsel in its many and varied expressions.

A Commitment

Our Lord closes his prayer with "Amen." This word comes from the Aramaic word AMENA, which means "faithful," "truthful," and "sincere." It also means "sealed in truth" and "trustworthy." This word means so much more than just "it is so" or "so be it," though these words do carry some of this meaning. When we say "Amen" to our prayers, we're each individually saying, "I'll back it up; everything I've said, I'll be faithful to."

In Jesus' day people didn't usually make written contracts; they made oral agreements. When they completed the agreement, they would say to each other, "Amen." Each one was saying to the other, "I'll keep my side of the bargain." The parties involved knew that they must be faithful to their oral contract and carry out all the things they had agreed to do.

So, "Amen" means a commitment. It means, "I'll be faithful to this." In saying "Amen," we are acknowledging our willingness to work with that which we have affirmed and for which we have prayed. We are believing that we will receive our requests.

Anything you pray for and ask, believe that you will receive it, and it will be done for you. (Mark 11:24)

The Final Attunement

Knowing that God, our loving Father, cares for us and desires only good for us, we can rest assured that He will keep His part of the agreement, for He never changes. Therefore, we, too, must be faithful to our part of the prayer.

Through this eighth attunement we are filling our hearts and minds with positive affirmations of the inexhaustible, unending supply of God which is in us and around us. We see and feel the guidance, the power, and the glory (riches) flowing through us and out from us. This is the final attunement.

10

WALK IN HIS WAY

As we have seen now, the admonition to pray "in Jesus' name" means that we should pray "in the manner" in which Jesus prayed when he communed with his Father. The manner in which he prayed was not one of begging, but one of acknowledgment and of a consciousness which is fully attuned to Truth.

When we understand this prayer, and are truly attuned to its meaning, our attitude is adjusted to Infinite Intelligence, to the true understanding of God, of man, and of the universe. Then our actions will spontaneously and naturally demonstrate our inner attunement with God.

Through this prayer—

We acknowledge and realize who God is—a loving Father Who is forever at hand and concerned about His children's welfare.

We acknowledge and realize who we are—children of a gracious Father who are provided for in all ways.

We acknowledge and accept God's Kingdom, ruling within our own hearts.

We acknowledge and realize that God always provides for His children, so we need not fear the future.

We acknowledge and understand the value of forgiveness, both for ourselves and for others, even as our loving Father forgives all who ask of Him.

We acknowledge and work with the guidance of our Father within, Who ever leads us away from error and toward Truth.

We acknowledge and believe that all will be accomplished because it is sealed in truth and in faithfulness.

Therefore, we acknowledge and accept only one Kingdom or Counsel, only one Power, and only one Glory—the Kingdom, the Power, and the Glory of our Loving Heavenly Father!

(Amen)

Rocco A. Errico, D.D., is a dynamic lecturer whose unique Near-Eastern approach to the Scriptures has made him one of the most sought-after speakers in the nation. He is an internationally known author, teacher, and scholar, whose work is based on Aramaic, the language of Jesus, and on the ancient Eastern culture which influenced the Biblical writers.

He has appeared on numerous radio and television talk shows and has been enthusiastically received. His outstanding scholarship, lively and humorous manner, and uncommon simplicity of expression have brought him ovations from audiences worldwide.

Dr. Errico is uniquely qualified to interpret Semitic thought, as he was personally taught the Aramaic language by the world-renowned Near-Eastern theologian, Biblical authority, and translator, Dr. George M. Lamsa. Dr. Errico is proficient in Old and

New Testament interpretation, Biblical history, culture and psychology.

Under the auspices of the Noohra Foundation of Santa Ana, California, Dr. Errico is now extending this new light nationwide. As Founder and President of this non-profit, educational organization, he speaks to church and civic groups, study groups and retreats, and colleges and universities throughout the country.

An ordained minister, Dr. Errico has served non-denominational churches in California and Texas. For over 25 years, he has functioned in the capacity of counselor, lecturer, teacher and practitioner of spiritual healing among many denominations. His travels have taken him throughout the United States, and to the British Isles, Ireland, Canada, Mexico, Europe and the Holy Land. He now devotes his full time to promoting the Aramaic teachings and Near-Eastern approach to the Scriptures.

In addition to his many other activities, Dr. Errico has translated the four Gospels into modern Spanish from Dr. Lamsa's English translation of the ancient Aramaic texts.

Interested groups are invited to contact the Noohra Foundation for more information on this new breakthrough in Biblical understanding. Arrangements for speaking by Dr. Errico may also be made through the Foundation.

NOOHRA FOUNDATION, INC.
18022 Cowan St., Suite 100B
Irvine, CA 92714
(714) 975-1944